# Folk Football

A few hundred years ago in England some villages an[d]
played a game of football between each other called folk
football. Folk football was also known as mob football,
medieval football or in some places as Shrovetide football.

This kind of football was nothing like the football we can see played
today by modern football clubs. In many cases, folk football would be
played by the whole town or village and involve an unlimited number
of players. Normally teams would have to get an inflated pig's bladder
to a marker at one end of the village to win the game.

Some of these early games with a ball still survive today in places like:
Alnwick, Northumberland, Ashbourne-Derbyshire shown below,
Atherstone-Warwickshire and Kirkwall-Orkney.

Other ball-based games
were played to local rules
across the United Kingdom
in the early 1800s. One
example of these games was
played in Edinburgh in 1824.
It involved kicking a ball over
an agreed line and also
involved teamwork, but it
was different to modern
football.

## 4 But the game we now play today is called association football so where did that come from?

### Sheffield Football Club

The oldest modern association football clubs were started in Sheffield from 1857 onwards. The very first modern football club, **Sheffield FC** was formed by two members of the Sheffield Cricket Club, see facing page.

In 1855, Sheffield Cricket Club moved into a brand-new sports and cricket ground called Bramall Lane. Bramall Lane is still there. It is now used as a football stadium by Sheffield United FC who formed in 1889. It held its first organised football match in 1862 when Sheffield FC played Hallam FC. This makes it the oldest surviving top-flight football stadium in the world.

Members of the Sheffield Cricket Club started to play 'knock-about' football in 1855 to keep playing sports together during the winter months when cricket wasn't played.

**Creswick**

**Prest**

**5**

**Nathaniel Creswick & William Prest**, two members of the Sheffield Cricket Club, formed **Sheffield FC** in 1857. The new club played at a ground near to Bramall Lane called East Bank. They didn't have strips but had **coloured caps** to tell which team they were playing for. The clubs' members played each other as there were no other clubs to play at the time.

**FIFA**, the people who now govern football across the world recognise **Sheffield FC** as the world's oldest association football club.

Many of the people who played very early for **Sheffield FC** had played games of football at their schools and universities. Some had been to Cambridge University,

others to schools such as Collegiate School in Sheffield, Penistone Grammar School near Sheffield & Rossall School in Fleetwood, Lancashire. All these places encouraged their students to play early forms of football.

# So where did the earliest Rules of football come from?

Soon after they started **Sheffield FC** in 1857, its members wrote some rules for the games they played.

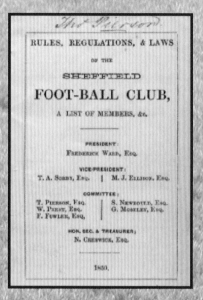

**Sheffield FC** members gathered rules from a variety of places and then by playing them, developed their own Sheffield football rules. The first version of the Sheffield rules was produced in October 1858.

These first Sheffield FC rules of the game were the first ever football rules written down by a modern football club.

**Sheffield FC's** early rules ended up being very similar to the game played by Cambridge University students at the time. You could not pick the ball up and run with it or seriously foul and injure other players.

The rules did not allow hacking or tripping your opponent. Hacking was a violent way of bringing your opponent down using your feet and legs and the Sheffield rules outlawed this way of playing.

In these first Sheffield rules you could catch the ball with your hands if the ball was in the air. This was called a 'fair catch'. After a fair catch you could not run with the ball but had to put it on the ground and take a free kick.

A fair charge was allowed in Sheffield rules but not in Cambridge rules. This was an important feature of football for many years and can sometimes be seen today-at the discretion of the referee.

The first Sheffield Rules were approved in the city's, Adelphi Hotel, on 28 October 1858. These rules and subsequent ones greatly influenced the modern game.

**7**

# Which rules and tactics of modern football came from Sheffield?

Many early rules and tactics that you have heard of today started in Sheffield. 11 a side, the 90 minutes a game, the ball size, free kicks, early form of penalties, **corner kicks**, passing, **the crossbar**, **heading** and referees all originally came from Sheffield's influence. Also, the rule about which team return the ball to play after it was kicked into touch came from Sheffield.

Ball size

Cross

Heading the Ball

Corner Kicks

In the early days of football there were often no fully agreed rules of the game. When a team visited another ground, they played by the rules of the home team which were often different to their own. As a result, disputes often happened about what was legal and what was not.

To avoid these problems a match played in 1866 at Battersea Park between the London FA and Sheffield agreed that there would be 11 v 11 players; the game would last 90 minutes; and a number 5 Lillywhite's ball would be used. Also, during a match, in early 1872, at The Oval in London, the home team and spectators were surprised to see the **Sheffielders heading the ball**. This was an innovation which continues today.

An early illustration showing a player heading the ball towards a goal where the goalposts have a crossbar

# When was the birth of the first Football Association?

On 26th October 1863 the Football Association formed and held their very first meeting at **The Freemason's Tavern** on Great Queens Street in central London.

The newly formed Football Association used the most recent versions of the Cambridge University and Sheffield rules to help form its own rules.

The Football Association was formed on the proposal of Ebenezer Cobb Morley at the Freemasons' Tavern, which stood on this site. The modern game of football was born on this day.

26 October 1863

It took six meetings to decide the new FA rules and before the fifth meeting **Sheffield FC's William Chesterman** had to write a letter to **Secretary E C Morley** to help convince the FA not to include running with the ball in your hands and hacking in its new code. He was successful and at the last meeting the FA's finally agreed rules did not include both being able to use your hands to run with the ball or hacking.

The new FA's rules below marked the moment in football history when football as we know it today started to become separate to rugby.

**Sheffield FC** joined the Football Association in 1863 and then helped to influence how the rules of the game developed for the next 14 years. In 1877 both sets of rules amalgamated to form the first ever universal codification of the rules of football. We still play by the latest version of these rules today. The rules that any association football club plays by today are a mixture of the original FA and Sheffield rules plus other rules that have been written since then.

**William Chesterman**

**Ebenezer Cobb Morley**

# Which club became the second oldest in the world?

Soon after **Sheffield FC** had formed, many other clubs started to form across the country, but before the mid-1870's nearly half of these clubs came from Sheffield.

The very first match between two clubs took place on 26th December 1860 at a ground in west Sheffield called Sandygate. **Hallam FC** had just formed as the world's second oldest modern organised football club and **Sheffield FC** decided to play **Hallam FC** in an organised match. This match is recognized by FIFA and Guinness Book of Records as the very first game between two modern football clubs ever.

The same match is also the oldest and first ever football derby since both clubs came from the same town/city.

Hallam FC playing at their Sandygate, Crosspool, Sheffield ground

Because both **Sheffield FC** and **Hallam FC** still exist as football clubs today, when they meet in a game, they still are playing a repeat of football's first ever club game and derby.

**Hallam FC** play at the Sandygate ground which you can still visit today. Sandygate is the oldest surviving football ground in the world that still hosts modern football matches.

**Hallam FC** was started by **John Charles Shaw** and **Captain Tom Vickers**. **Vickers** had left **Sheffield FC** after a disagreement with Nathaniel Creswick.

**John Charles Shaw** came to Sheffield from the football mad school called Penistone Grammar School. Penistone is a small town just northwest of Sheffield where many early influential footballers came from. **J. C. Shaw** joined **Sheffield FC** before he set up **Hallam FC** and was a very influential in early Sheffield's football history as we shall see later.

John Charles Shaw
founder of Hallam FC

Image by Lucy Pimpernel Wood

# What happened next? - Sheffield the first city of football

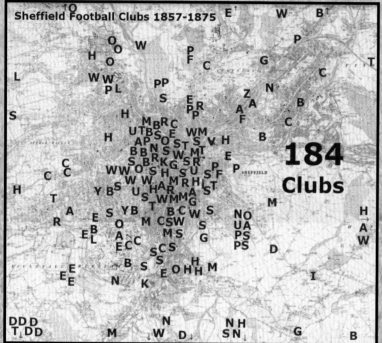

Sheffield Football Clubs 1857-1875

184 Clubs

## Origins of Football Clubs (1857 to 1875)

- Sheffield — 49%
- South East England — 21%
- East Midlands — 9%
- Shrop/Staff/Chesh — 6%
- Lancashire — 4%
- Other — 11%

By March 1875 Sheffield had nearly half of all the football clubs in the world, at least 184 of them in total. Sheffield had only 1% of the country's population but nearly half of all the clubs that had ever existed. It had the world's first ever footballing sub-culture.

Some of these clubs had familiar Sheffield names like **Norton FC, Walkley New Connexion FC, Handsworth FC, Ecclesfield FC, Heeley FC, Loxley FC.** Plus others with stranger names such as **Thursday Wanderers FC, Mount Tabor FC, Pitsmoor FC, Zulus FC, Deep Pits FC,** and **Good Intent FC.**

# How did the world's first ever cup tournaments happen?

There were enough clubs in Sheffield in 1867 for them to form their own county association. This was the world's first county football association.

Also, in 1867 some of the Sheffield clubs took part in the world's first ever football tournament for a trophy called the **Youdan Cup**.

Thomas Youdan was a local theatre owner who organised the tournament.

The final of the Youdan Cup took place at Bramall Lane in front of 3000 spectators. **Hallam** beat **Norfolk** and **John Shaw**, image on page 13, from Penistone, captain and founder of the world's second oldest football club Hallam FC, lifted the world's first ever football trophy. This trophy can still be seen at Hallam FCs ground on Sandygate Road, Crosspool, Sheffield.

Youdan Cup

Cromwell Cup

**16** A year later in 1868 another trophy tournament was held called the **Cromwell Cup** and this was won by **The Wednesday** (later known as **Sheffield Wednesday**). **John Marsh**, also from Penistone and captain of **The Wednesday** lifted the world's second oldest football trophy.

In 1871, four years after the Youdan Cup in Sheffield, the Football Association started its own cup tournament called the **FA Cup** which is still played for today.

Sheffield also has the fifth oldest cup competition and the oldest county association cup, the **Sheffield FA Senior Cup** of 1876.

Also from Sheffield came the oldest charity association cup, the **Wharncliffe Cup** 1878.

Sheffield & Hallamshire Senior Cup

The Original FA Cup

Wharncliffe Cup

# The Clegg Shield

This beautiful old trophy has been played for and won by a Sheffield secondary school every year since 1889. The very first winners of

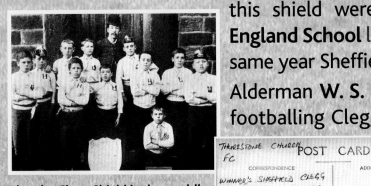

this shield were **Thurlstone Church of England School** left, in 1889. This was also the same year Sheffield United were formed.

Alderman **W. S. Clegg**, father of the famous footballing Clegg brothers paid to have the shield made as he thought it was a good idea to help the young school boys keep fit and competitive.

**Also the Clegg Shield is the world's second oldest schools trophy**

*THURLSTONE CHURCH FC*
*POST CARD*
*CORRESPONDENCE*
*WINNER'S SHEFFIELD CLEGG SHEILD 1889 WITHOUT A GOAL SCORED AGAINTS THEM.*
*ADDRESS ONLY*

A world cup winner, full England internationals and many local footballing legends have all played in the Clegg Shield Competition.

Clegg Shield Winners Medal presented to F Lavender captain of All Saints CE School 1906

Clegg Shield

# Sheffield's world footballing firsts

From Sheffield's football culture we have many world's firsts, the first matches, derbies, stadiums, and grounds. Sheffield also had the first church club (Cemetery Road Church FC); club from a factory works (Lockwood Brothers FC); club from a hotel **(York Hotel FC)** pictured below; club from a pub (Garrick FC) and club from a state school (All Saints Night School FC). Sheffield had the first clubs of these types of clubs that had formed anywhere in the world.

The York Hotel, Broomhill

## A list of some of Sheffield's main footballing firsts are:

**1857** The oldest football club: Sheffield FC

**1858** The first modern football club rules

**1860** The oldest football ground: Sandygate

**1860** The first ever official club match
Sheffield FC vs Hallam FC

**1860** The world's first ever football derby
Sheffield FC vs Hallam FC

**1861** The first ever charity match
Sheffield vs Hallam

**1862** The oldest topflight football stadium
Bramall Lane

**1865** The first match between two towns
Sheffield versus Nottingham

**1867** The first ever football tournament
and trophy, The Youdan Cup

1867 The first county FA, Sheffield FA

1868 The first ever golden goal  Cromwell Cup

1869 The first club from a Catholic Church - St Vincent's

1876 The first professional player: Jimmy Lang

1878 The first use of Floodlights: Bramall Lane

## More about Sheffield's influence on association football

Some other significant contributions from Sheffield:

1857 the oldest club house

1861 first charity game

1862 first club called United

1867 oldest County association

1867 the first use of referees

1867 first playoff match

1872 made the first ever FA cup

1889 the joint oldest schools FA

1893 made the first ever FA Amateur Cup

1923 the penalty box D

1927 the first radio broadcast

1992 the first Premier League goal scored by Brian Deane pictured of Sheffield United FC

Sheffield was also involved in the first ever matches between two towns or cities.  From the mid 1860's onwards Sheffield teams played teams from other cities such as Nottingham, London, Lincoln, Birmingham, and Glasgow.

# Sheffield's historic football grounds & stadiums

Sheffield has and had some of the most historic football ground locations in the world. **Bramall Lane,** is the oldest stadium in the world to host topflight football, since it has been hosting modern football matches since 1862. It also hosted 3 of the 5 first ever football tournament cup finals, Youdan Cup (1867), Cromwell Cup (1868) & Sheffield FA Cup (1877). The stadium was also where the first ever floodlit game happened in 1878. You can still visit Bramall Lane in Sheffield as it is now used by professional football team, Sheffield United FC.

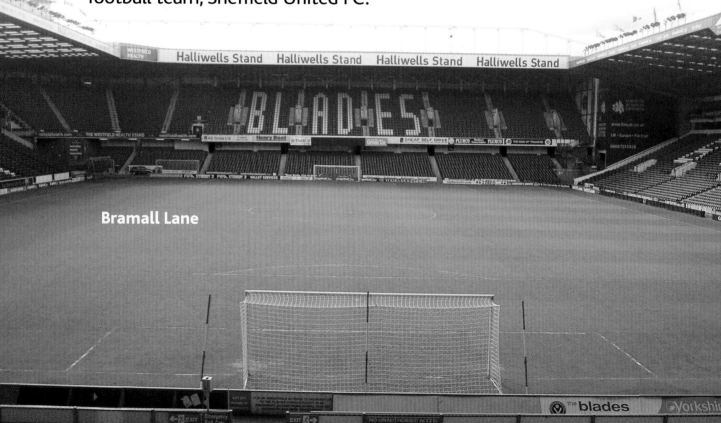

Bramall Lane

# Sheffield's historic grounds

**Olive Grove** was very close to where Sheffield FC started. The ground at East Bank was the first permanent home of The Wednesday from 1887 to 1889. The first match at the ground took place on 12th September 1887 against Blackburn Rovers and ended in a 4-4 draw. Sheffield's famous England international Billy Mosforth played for The Wednesday in this first Olive Grove game.

On 15th December 1890 the first ever Steel City Derby took place at Olive Grove between The Wednesday & Sheffield United.

Olive Grove

# Sheffield's historic grounds

**22** Hyde Park, right, in Sheffield was an old cricket ground, but it was also sometimes used for important football matches. In 1861 the world's very first charity game took place at Hyde Park between Sheffield FC and Hallam FC. This game was played to raise money for a new Sheffield hospital.

Sandygate, below, **home of Hallam FC is the oldest surviving football ground in the world.** The ground hosted the first ever match played between two clubs on 26th December 1860. In 1867 it was one of the venues used for the world's first ever football tournament, the Youdan Cup. On 16th February 1867 Hallam FC played & beat Heeley FC at Sandygate to give birth to tournament football.

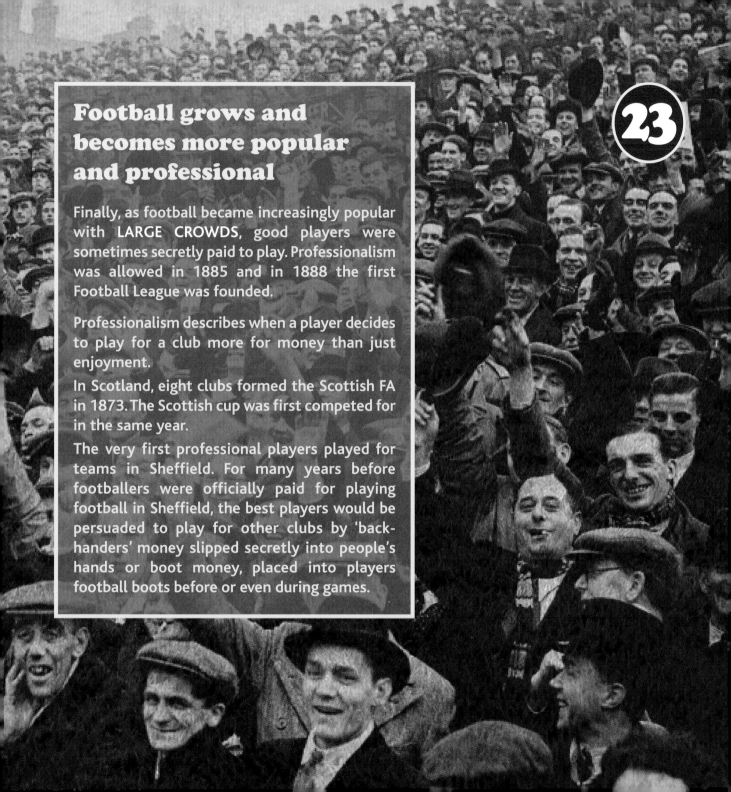

# Football grows and becomes more popular and professional

Finally, as football became increasingly popular with **LARGE CROWDS**, good players were sometimes secretly paid to play. Professionalism was allowed in 1885 and in 1888 the first Football League was founded.

Professionalism describes when a player decides to play for a club more for money than just enjoyment.

In Scotland, eight clubs formed the Scottish FA in 1873. The Scottish cup was first competed for in the same year.

The very first professional players played for teams in Sheffield. For many years before footballers were officially paid for playing football in Sheffield, the best players would be persuaded to play for other clubs by 'back-handers' money slipped secretly into people's hands or boot money, placed into players football boots before or even during games.

# The Birth of the People's Game

**24** Some of Sheffield's best Victorian footballers could not understand why they could not earn money from their talent. Unlike public school educated wealthy gentlemen they were too poor to be able to play for fun if they did not have a job.

**Jack Hunter** was a brilliant footballer who could play in any position. He was so good that he became the first working class footballer to captain the England football team. He was playing for **Heeley FC** at the time, but he also played for **The Wednesday**.

Hunter and some other players set up a team called the Sheffield Zulus, to play games in Sheffield and other towns to raise money for men injured in the Zulu wars in 1879.

Out of money raised from selling tickets they paid themselves expenses to cover travel costs, accommodation, and food. This made them unpopular with Mr Pierce-Dix who was the secretary of the Sheffield Football Association. He insisted that the Zulus disband in 1882 because earning money from playing football was not in the spirit of the game and not allowed in the rules.

Illustration of
Jack Hunter
in his ZULU kit

Jack Hunter was very unhappy about his treatment by the Sheffield FA and decided to try his luck in Lancashire where professionalism was tolerated. He joined **Blackburn Olympic FC**, rather than the slightly bigger Blackburn Rovers team on the promise that the chairman, a factory owner, would buy him a pub in return for him taking a job as player coach.

The chairman had a dream. He wanted **Blackburn Olympic FC** to win the 1883 FA Cup. The FA Cup had been dominated by elite teams from London who were former pupils of famous public schools like Eton, Harrow, and Charterhouse. They had all the advantages of privilege. They could attend the best gymnasiums, afford the best quality food, and be assured of a good night's sleep every night.

Many of the Lancashire mill workers in the **Blackburn Olympic FC** team were less fortunate than their public-school rivals. They had to work hard in difficult conditions, and many lived in damp and unsanitary housing.

It appeared unlikely that they would ever be able to challenge the bigger, faster, and stronger upper-class gentlemen.

Blackburn Olympic FC
Jack Hunter can be seen centre row with arm on teammates shoulder.
Also the FA Cup Final Winners Medal 1883

**26** However, Hunter had a cunning plan. He persuaded the chairman to pay for a week at the seaside, where Hunter's players enjoyed the sea air and, more importantly, were taught a tactic new to Lancashire.

Instead of dribbling the ball until possession was lost, Hunter taught the Olympic players to use short passes, move and keep possession. Long passes to each wing followed by crosses would confuse the gentlemen team who were used to charging in a pack, straight up the middle.

After a long series of games they destroyed the ex-FA Cup winners, **Old Carthusians** 4-0 in the semi-final and then shocked the world by defeating the mighty **Old Etonians** in the final.

Everyone agreed that the biggest giant killing shock in football history was down to the coaching of one man-Sheffield's **Jack Hunter**.

**Jack's team Heeley FC** are reported using the same tactics many years earlier in a game against another top Sheffield team, **Sheffield Albion**.

The 1883 FA Cup Final was one of the most important matches in football history. Football was never the same again. From now on it was the people's game and provincial and Northern teams would go on to dominate English football. Jack, later went on to become trainer to **Blackburn Rovers FC**

**Blackburn Rovers FC,**
**Jack, then club trainer, on extreme right**
T Brandon seated centre also
played for The Wednesday

# The Billy Mosforth story

Back home in Sheffield some people were suggesting that, if **Jack Hunter** had not been forced to leave Sheffield to have a professional career in Blackburn, then The Wednesday might have been the first Northern team to win the FA Cup.

A player called **Billy Mosforth**, pictured below in his **Albion FC** kit, was one of the greatest players Sheffield has ever produced. He joined other Sheffield players in a team called **Sheffield Rovers**. Billy Mosforth, Sheffield born and bred, was so good that he was once carried off the field by Scottish fans at Hampden Park! Imagine that happening today? Billy played for numerous Sheffield based clubs.

Sheffield players wanted to play in the FA Cup. It was a more important competition than the Football League in its day, and when The Wednesday failed to get their FA cup registration in on time, some of The Wednesday players moved to a team called **Lockwood Brothers**, who in 1887, came close to winning the FA Cup themselves and would probably have reached the final if they had not been victims of a refereeing error against the famous **West Bromwich Albion**.

They then decided that they would start a new team called **Sheffield Rovers**. Rovers would pay money to attract the best players in Sheffield and they wanted to win the FA Cup.

After this The Wednesday decided that they had no choice but to fully turn professional, they were the first senior club in Sheffield to do so, and, in 1896 they won the FA Cup, beating Wolverhampton Wanderers 2-1 at Crystal Palace.

# Sir John Charles Clegg

**28**

**John Charles Clegg** was an English footballer and later both chairman and president of **The Football Association**. He was born in Sheffield and lived there his whole life. He competed in the first international match between England and Scotland in 1872. He was the older brother of William Clegg, another early England International, with whom he played both with and against.

He became heavily involved in local football serving as chairman and president of **The Wednesday** and was one of the founders of **Sheffield United**. He won one cap for England.

He played a critical role in merging the two competing Sheffield football associations into the **Sheffield and Hallamshire Football Association**, of which he then became chairman. During his reign in charge of the FA he became known as the Napoleon of Football.

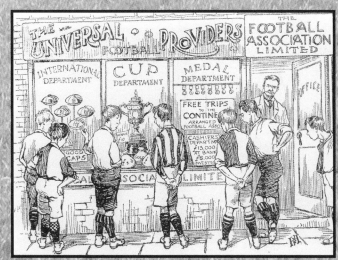

Cartoon detailing Clegg as FA chairman telling the young players the error of their ways by not joining his cup competitions
From Yorkshire Newspaper 1907

# Sir William Edwin Clegg

**William Edwin Clegg** was the younger brother of John Charles Clegg with whom he played at **The Wednesday**. The two were the first brothers to both be capped for England, although they never played in the same International match.

He was described as being "a safe kick and good half-back" in Charles Alcock's 1875 edition of the Football Annual. He won two caps for England.

After retiring from football through injury, he continued within the game as an administrator and became president of **The Wednesday** and vice president of **Sheffield and Hallamshire Football Association**.

**William Clegg** became a solicitor. His most notable case was when he represented the notorious criminal/murderer **Charles Peace**. William was

only 27 when he defended **Peace**. On the morning of the day the case came to court, William was playing in an important football match but still managed to address the court trial on time.

The Clegg brothers welcoming Sheffield Football Club back home after their 1904 Amateur Cup win

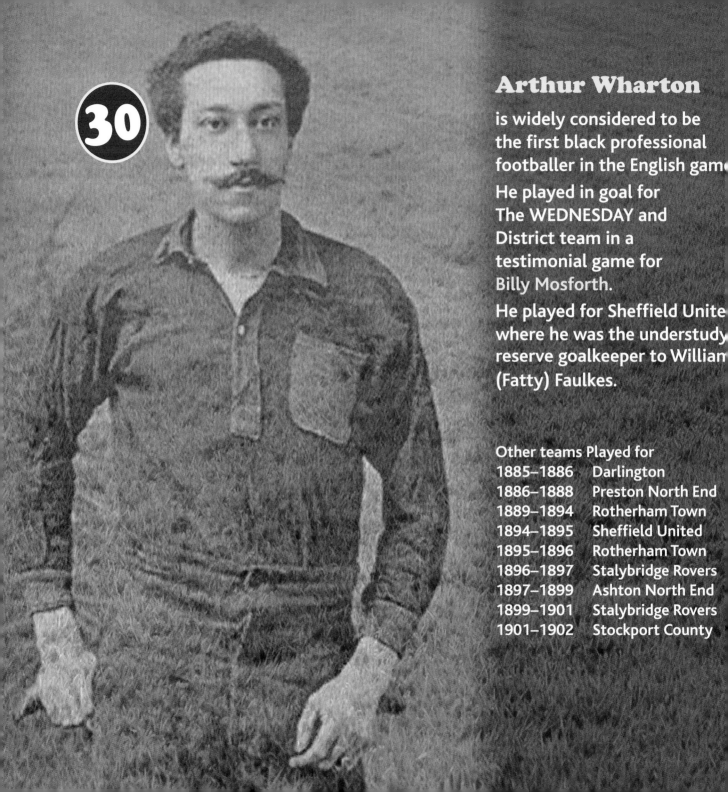

**30**

# Arthur Wharton

is widely considered to be the first black professional footballer in the English game.

He played in goal for The WEDNESDAY and District team in a testimonial game for Billy Mosforth.

He played for Sheffield United where he was the understudy reserve goalkeeper to William (Fatty) Faulkes.

Other teams Played for
1885–1886    Darlington
1886–1888    Preston North End
1889–1894    Rotherham Town
1894–1895    Sheffield United
1895–1896    Rotherham Town
1896–1897    Stalybridge Rovers
1897–1899    Ashton North End
1899–1901    Stalybridge Rovers
1901–1902    Stockport County

# SHEFFIELD
## A History of the first city of Football

In 1904 Sheffield Football Club won the F.A. Amateur Cup
against Ealing FC with over 6,000 spectators turning up to watch.
Sheffield FC 3 Ealing FC 1.

# But what about the Women?

**32** Girls have always played football, and many loved the game. Some featured in strong primary school teams over the years. Others have become expert coaches and referees.

The first women's teams appeared in the 1880's and there were games in South Yorkshire during the subsequent decade. During the First World War, when many women did important work in steel and munition factories it became very popular. Shortly after the war teams such as **Dick Kerr Ladies** (below) from Preston became extremely popular.

Many of the games were played to raise money for charities and elderly upper middle-class men who ran football became worried that they were raising money for left wing groups that might take over the country. They were also concerned that it was 'unwomanly' to play football and they cruelly decided to act and ban women from playing on FA affiliated grounds. After the ban girls were not encouraged to play in schools, were not taught the rules and for several generations had no female role models.

Dick Kerr Ladies

In banning women from playing on FA affiliated grounds they effectively banned women's football.

Vickers Ltd., ladies football team helped to raise money for the wounded soldiers fund

This terrible rule was not removed until 1970, almost fifty years later. Generations of women were unable to play the game they loved. It remains one of the most shameful decisions in football history.

It is only in the last few years that women have played in the finest stadiums in the country. After England's victory in the Women's Euros in 2022 (with a wonderful semi-final played at Bramall Lane against Sweden) women's football became hugely popular in England, and Sheffield's **Millie Bright**, seen celebrating below, was awarded an OBE. With more girls in the United Kingdom playing football, the future is bright indeed!

**UEFA Women's EURO 2022 Champions**

Millie Bright

England Squad
1966 World Cup
Winners

# A Global Game

In the late 1800s many new association football clubs formed across the world in many different countries.

Railway workers from the British Isles who worked abroad in places like South America helped to spread the game and introduced football to the people in other countries.

In 1904 FIFA was formed to govern world football.

In 1930 FIFA held it's very first world cup tournament in Uruguay. See next page.

Association football was now a global game loved by the whole world, played by many different groups of people.

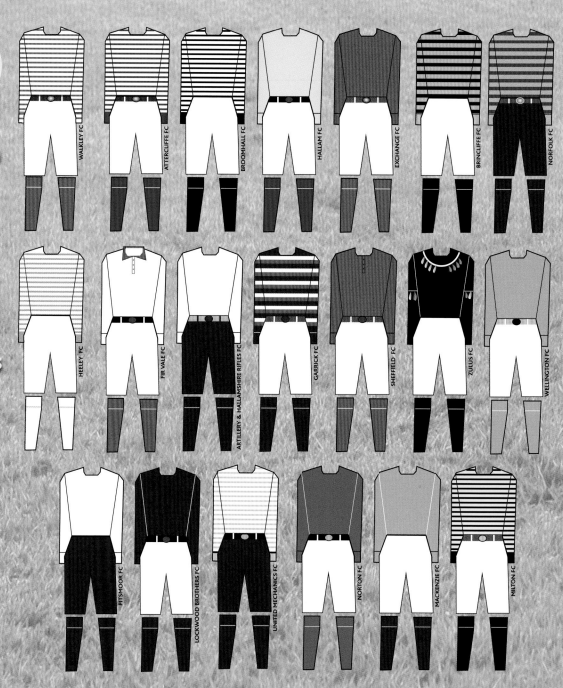

**36**

Some of the strips worn by the early Sheffield local football teams formed around 1857-1875

WALKLEY FC
ATTERCLIFFE FC
BROOMHALL FC
HALLAM FC
EXCHANGE FC
BRINCLIFFE FC
NORFOLK FC
HEELEY FC
FIR VALE FC
ARTILLERY & HALLAMSHIRE RIFLES FC
GARRICK FC
SHEFFIELD FC
ZULUS FC
WELLINGTON FC
PITSMOOR FC
LOCKWOOD BROTHERS FC
UNITED MECHANICS FC
NORTON FC
MACKENZIE FC
MILTON FC

# FIFA World Cups

| | | |
|---|---|---|
| 2022 Qatar | **Argentina** | 3-3, then Argentina defeated France 4-2 in penalties |
| 2018 Russia | **France** | France 4-2 Croatia |
| 2014 Brazil | **Germany** | Germany 1-0 Argentina |
| 2010 South Africa | **Spain** | Spain 1-0 Netherlands |
| 2006 Germany | **Italy** | 1-1, then Italy beat France 5-3 in penalties |
| 2002 Korea & Japan | **Brazil** | Brazil 2-0 Germany |
| 1998 France | **France** | France 3-0 Brazil |
| 1994 USA | **Brazil** | 0-0, then Brazil defeated Italy 3-2 in penalties |
| 1990 Italy | **Germany** | Germany 1-0 Argentina |
| 1986 Mexico | **Argentina** | Argentina 3-2 Germany |
| 1982 Spain | **Italy** | Italy 3-1 Germany |
| 1978 Argentina | **Argentina** | Argentina 3-1 Holland |
| 1974 Germany | **Germany** | Germany 2-1 Holland |
| 1970 Mexico | **Brazil** | Brazil 4-1 Italy |
| 1966 England | **ENGLAND** | England 4-2 Germany |
| 1962 Chile | **Brazil** | Brazil 3-1 Czechoslovakia |
| 1958 Sweden | **Brazil** | Brazil 5-2 Sweden |
| 1954 Switzerland | **Germany** | Germany 3-2 Hungary |
| 1950 Brazil | **Uruguay** | Uruguay 2-1 Brazil |
| 1942-1946 | not held | |
| 1938 France | **Italy** | Italy 4-2 Hungary |
| 1934 Italy | **Italy** | Italy 2-1 Czechoslovakia |
| 1930 Uruguay | **Uruguay** | Uruguay 4-2 Argentina |

## 38 Today almost every country on the planet has some form of football league system consisting of professional and amateur clubs.

* There are nearly 4,500 professional clubs.

* 240 million registered players.

* 211 FIFA member countries in 6 regional confederations

* Over 130,000 registered professional football players

* Over 1 billion people watched the 2023 Women's World Cup tournament on TV

* FIFA estimate there are currently over 5 billion football fans across the world.

* Strongly influenced by Sheffield from 1857, football truly now is the world's biggest and most popular sport.

**Wembley Stadium**

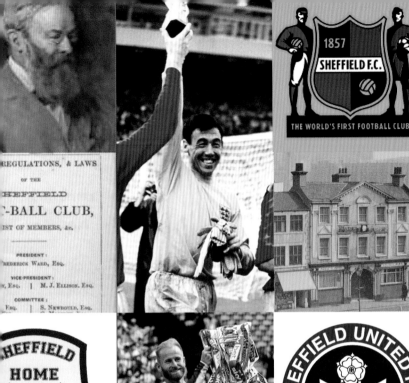

SHEFFIELD F.C.
1857
THE WORLD'S FIRST FOOTBALL CLUB

**39**

SHEFFIELD
HOME
OF
FOOTBALL
#THEWORLDSFIRST

SHEFFIELD UNITED F.C.
1889

18 60
HALLAM F.C.

**SHEFFIELD**
**is the Home**
**of Football**

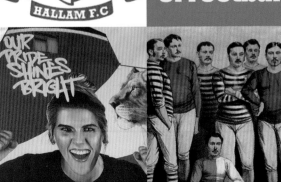

CONSILIO ET ANIMIS

All rights reserved & copyright
Sheffield Home of Football 2024
Sheffield Home of Football is a registered Charity No: 1204425
Company number CE033304

This book Compiled/Written by
Stephen T. Wood
John Stocks, John P. Wilson
Layout & Design Mike Liversidge
Printed by Pickards design & print
sheffieldhomeoffootball.org

ISBN 978-1-3999-8857-5